STREET FOOD & SPICE

Adam Melius

FAITH MAKES THINGS POSSIBLE NOT EASY

CONTENTS

DEDICATION

I dedicate this book to my friend Carlos who died earlier this year.
Thank you for starting my career. You were one of the few people that wanted to see me succeed and always overextended yourself to help me out. Thankyou
R.I.P

ACKNOWLEDGEMENTS

First and foremost, I thank God for allowing me to achieve the things I have achieved. On my own I could not have done half the things I have done. But through God doors have opened that I didn't even know were there.

I would like to say a huge thank you to my wife Laura for supporting all that I have done over the last 15 years. I accredit everything to you. I extend a similar thankyou to my children, parents and grandparents. Thank you for being the best motivation for success that I could have asked for

It is often easy to overlook all the staff I have employed since starting out on my own. In short without you there would be no me. Without the efforts you all made with our clients, customers and one another the business wouldn't have grown the way it has. You have all made a huge effort to embrace the ethos of the company and to excel when I have been absent. Thank you so much for sticking with me and thank you for keeping me young.
"Thanks for today"

I owe a huge thankyou to Joshua Parry & Naeem Bhunnoo. You guys have been outstanding sous chefs. Your food has played a big part in the development of the company. Thank you for your loyalty and the efforts you have made to drive the company forward

Finally, if you are a customer or client or anyone that has retained our services or purchased food from us before "Thankyou" Your sales have all contributed to keeping the company sustainable
Thanks again

YOUR TWO-PART COOKERY COURSE

Street Food & Spice & Comfort & Classics

Both books are incredibly different. The first book revolves solely around the chili. Its detailed recipes that you will need to think about before you cook and explores half of my food culture.

The second makes life a bit easier for the newfound foodie. It goes deep into my original cooking experiences as a chef and really shows how great British food can be. It Also explores the other half of my food culture

INTRODUCTION

Like most self-taught chefs my story starts at the bottom. It was by default and what seemed like bad luck at the time that I stumbled across this amazing industry.

At the age of 15 I took my first weekend job in the British home stores kitchen in Sutton. At the time the minimum wage was less than £5.00 per hour. But to me this was good money I was happy, and I won't have to take my work home with me. My best friend Daniel worked at Matalan on the high street and I knew I would be able to meet him on my lunch breaks or if I decided to sneak out early. I was winning. On my first day of work I recall putting on a bright blue polo shirt with BHS embroidered in gold followed by a black baseball hat and being led from the staff room to the kitchen. I was thinking, this is great I am going to learn how to be a chef. Who knows I might end up running all their kitchens, hey I could even end up a CEO, stranger things have happened right? By the time I had finished daydreaming I was standing in a room with a wall to wall industrial dish washer, trollies of plates covered in half eaten food, dirty tea pots on top of one another, buckets and buckets of dirty cutlery and the room smelled like every possible smell you can imagine.

Ok so I have to work my way up I can do that, I got this. I remember thinking as I pushed a trolly full of crockery from my dishwash room to the other end of the kitchen, how do they do all this? I couldn't even begin to fathom the science involved. From taking an ingredient that is potentially harmful in its raw form and not just making it digestible to the human body, but edible and desirable. It interested me so much. So, I started looking at other restaurants and other menus. It was soon apparent that the world of food extends much further than BHS Sutton. I got a note pad and took notes on anything food related I saw. I brought cookbooks and kept recipe cuttings.

About 2 years later it was time to start college. I was going to Kingston college to study media production. No more wild dreams of becoming a chef or the CEO of British home stores. Looks like it's time to be a camera man, I know exciting!

Food is just an integral part of my family. The atmosphere and noise of everyone gathered around a table eating, laughing sharing stories. This is where I learned that good food is more than just good food. It really is the love behind it. It brings everyone together with a mutual need, food. In the hope that it creates mutual enjoyment. A table of good food is a game changer! It the experiences it leaves behind. I often recall Christmas day at my grandparents. I didn't really like turkey, but we looked forward to it because of the experiences that come with it. Laughing, joking and sharing stories. Maybe it's just me but I can always taste if a meal has been cooked with love.

Skipping forward 4 years I was 21. I had left Kingston collage and was now studying at the London electronics collage; I know another Long story. Alongside this I was working a part time job with an agency doing anything they wanted and going anywhere they wanted. I only had a few months left then I would be qualified. The phone rang "Abby" from employment plus, as per another job no one wants to do, hay ho think of the money I said. She said it was working on the bill (a big ITV drama at the time). On the bus on my way there I was thinking, well this is it, chances are ill be involved in a love scene with Polly, and I will be a big time actor by the end of the week. Hey if I tell them all about my media production course chances are ill be the CEO of the show (whatever that is) best not tell them I failed, hay stranger things have happened. As I walked up to the gate I thought, this doesn't look like much of a film set. Perhaps the cameras are hidden. A young lady on the desk said to go out back and ask for Alistair. I was over an hour late (as per my style at the time) so I went in for the double handshake "Adam Melius' I said with extra enthusiasm. He didn't even look me completely ignored me and shook my hand whilst continuing doing whatever he was doing. Not because I was late to be fair, I was just irrelevant. Certainly not the Stephen Spielberg I was expecting to meet.

He led me over to a box that had been turned upside down and made into a chair. He then placed boxes of dirty plates in front of me. I couldn't even process that fact that I was sitting on a wet box in my new Levi jeans and my Nike TNs have a slice rotten of tomato on them.

I looked up and I was in a circle of around 20 people. All sitting on makeshift chairs washing plates in boxes of water that was stone cold. Then a lorry arrived and started unloading more plates and cutlery. What a nightmare, I was sitting in a yard in Wimbledon thinking BHS was better and that was 4 years ago. After 20 minutes I broke away for a cigarette behind a mobile kitchen. I noticed a route out without anyone seeing me. Not that they would notice there was too much happening, and Alistair was so rude he didn't deserve a goodbye.

I put my Nike drawstring bag on and made a beeline for the gate dodging the mountains of different sized plate boxes, vans and lorries. I was out of sight, nearly at the end of the driveway just a few steps away. Then the office door opened on the right-hand side of me and a guy stepped out and said "Do you drive kidda" I replied "yes" reluctantly but I don't have a car, (another long story) that's ok I got the van. There it is the yes that defied my career. Two seconds later and who knows I would have left Woodhall Catering and completed college. I got in the driver's seat of a van twice the size of anything I had driven before. With the guy who stopped me "Carlos". He was a general manager alongside Alistair. Both of which became great friends of mine for years to come. Carlos especially made an effort to take me under his wing and ensure I always had work and learned along the way. But from there on it was a chef's life for me.

A photo taken around the time I joined Woodhall Catering

    I spent the next 7 years working for Woodhall Catering mainly cooking for tv and film productions and large-scale catering events. I ended up working with so many different chefs from so many different backgrounds. I became a sponge absorbing everything, taking notes on dishes, cooking methods, suppliers, costings, logistics the whole 9 yards. It was the best accidental apprenticeship I could ever imagine. The hours were insane 6-7 days a week 16 hours a day sometimes more. I was working with a different chef
    most days all with different methods and different skill sets. So, what the money was good, and the experience was priceless, and I wasn't washing up for Abby anymore. I was part of the team and I quickly gained a versatile knowledge of food and finally I had discovered a work ethic.

Someone said to me one day why don't you start your own catering business. I couldn't think of any reason why not. I actually remember being at a loss for words when asked. From that evening onwards I set my sites on my own catering company. I started sounding out this idea with Carlos, Alistair, Miranda, Mark and any chef who would listen.

It wasn't until 9 years later that I broke off and started my own Catering company. My motivation came from seeing the achievements of other company owners and with the experience I had behind me there was nothing stopping me.

At first, I still had to work alongside other companies whilst starting out. I still had to find a source of income whilst the company grew. So, I joined another agency and started freelancing various kitchens around London and surrey. Working with some real talents the quality of food I was producing with high and complicated. After a few more years I had a big enough client base to drop the freelancing and go full time working for myself. Don't get me wrong it was tough, good staff were hard to find, clients only wanted to use established companies and the equipment I needed was starting to prove costly. Like most small business owners, I had to figure out Tax, employment law, VAT, invoicing and gross profit margins. It was almost too much to deal with.

Time, prayer and a few mistakes later hear we are. I now have medium sized business with a strong structure. We were running Weddings, events, Tv & Film Locations for up to 200 people. Some weeks we would serve up to ten thousand meals. We were the contract caterer for 3 sports clubs and 3 pubs alongside the events. I think at its peak there was 30 employees at one time. Along with a few contractors.

Believe it or not at the start of 2020 me and a friend actually went back and brought the recruitment company that I originally started out working for. There was no more Abby, but she did leave a few things behind. Indirectly I ended up owing her a thank you, the same agency that had played a part in setting my business up then went on to set me up to buy them.

It doses all sound a bit easy when said like that, but there were scars. That's 30 different personalities, 30 different phone calls, 30 times a day, 30 days a month. It was potentially the toughest and the most rewarding thing I have ever done. The initial break to work full time for myself was hard, The people that were capable of helping me weren't willing, the chefs I wanted to work with were too busy or working for my newfound competitors.

Then I decided it was time to go to college. The business was relatively self-sufficient, and I had always said that when the time is right, I will qualify as a chef.

That was a fantastic experience meeting other chefs from other areas studying their food and watching them study mine. Couldn't believe I put it off for so long. The experience I had gained prior defiantly made it easier but another whole new way of working had just opened up to me.

Now a fully qualified chef I said to myself again what's next. "Street Food" I brought a mobile trailer and titled it "Street Food & Spice" with the concept of creating dishes that revolve around the chili. I had done so much with classic and gastro cuisine it was time to explore the hype around street food.

The theory was to apply Classic French practices and presentation to street food and bring some refinement to it. I didn't want to just limit it to street food there are so many traditional spice dishes that don't get the commercial success they should. Jerk Pork, Bezule, Panchito and salt cod fritters. The next 2 years were a blur of scotch bonnets, tagine pots, lemongrass & kaffir limes. Hay some things aren't meant to be refined some dishes are simple and best left that way. The ones that could be refined I did refine. All of a sudden food had a whole new level that I needed to explore.

It was 4 solid years of personal study again, note pad after not pad, sifting through old cuttings researching the genesis of each ingredient, and traveling as far as my wallet would allow me.

I took the opportunity to use one of the kitchens we rented within the company to develop over 250 authentic recipes. That would fall under "Street Food & Spice" It took a lot to cut the list down but eventually I did.

So, hear it is the tried and tested pain staking recipes that I am so happy to share with you. Both books are very different. Street food and spice is for the foodie, for those that don't need to be told to add salt to a dish and if they should add oil to the pan. It is deliberately vague leaving plenty to the imagination.

Prepare your pallet for a great journey. Enjoy

Shopping

Some of the ingredients in this book aren't always that easy to find. You sometimes have to venture further afield than usual. There are a few places below that I can recommend. A lot of our supplies require memberships however the ones below are open to anyone and everyone It is always worth searching thoroughly through your local supermarket these days they seem to have more than they used to and if you go from store to store products do vary

Food World - 117-119 London road, Mitcham, Cr4 2ja
Great for Indian and Caribbean spices and sauces. It also has a wide range of frozen fish and an exotic fruits and vegetables section.

Hoo Hing – Bond road, Mitcham, Cr4 3eb
This place specialises in Chinese food ingredients, you can get live crabs and lobster there. There is even a small canteen there. The broths there are really good! It mainly sells frozen products and spices and sauces

Korea Foods - Wyverm industrial estate. Unit 4-5, Beverley way, New Malden, Kt3 4ph
Hear you will find a really wide range of Korean spices. It has a Korean cake deli, live fish, butchery, fresh vegetables and a handful of spices that are not Korean but the majority if authentic Korean produce.

Wing Yip - 544 Purley way London, Cr0 4nz
This supermarket has a few restaurants attached along with a bakery. Huge range of frozen foods and ready meals. Some good sauces and fresh produce all at reasonable prices.

Serans - 147-149 Stafford road, Wallington, Sm6 9bn
Mainly Indian and some Indo/Asian spices hear. They have a really vast range and some hard to find products are usually in store

Four Brothers Super Store -1439 London road, Norbury, Sw16 4aq
I use this store for most my spices and fruit and veg. They have a huge range of Caribbean spice especially and loads of Asian ones as well. There is a butchery section along with loads of fresh fruit and vegetables as well

Holland Bazaar -1 Beddington cross, Croydon, Cr0 4xh
Hollands bazaar is open 24 hours a day. It is predominantly wholesale but has a good range of single sale items as well. The fruit and vegetable section in HUGE and worth checking out. Dry spices are mainly Turkish and eastern European is available

D. Parker & Sons butchers - 4 central avenue, Wallington, Sm6 8nx
We have used parkers as our primary butcher for the last 5 years. The quality, service and range are amazing even some of the most exotic cuts of meat they will find for you. Certainly, worth giving them a call

Fresh Food To You - https://freshfood2u.co (Completely Online)
This site delivers right from the supplier to your door. Usually a next day delivery, Great range, of fresh and dry goods without having to leave the house.

The Craft Kitchen - https://www.thecraftkitchen.co.uk (Online) delivery & collection
This is one of my company brands. It is an online shop that sells chef quality ready meals, sauces and marinades. Some of the recipes from these books are actually available on there. Whilst we don't sell the raw ingredients, we make the food to order when you order

Uptown Flava - https://www.uptownflava.co.uk (Online) delivery & collection

One of the other brands we have for foodies is Uptown Flava. An artisan free range fried chicken takeaway. Sold indoors and available on deliveroo & uber eats. All fresh using locally sourced ingredients. Available hot and in DIY Kits

POULTRY

JERK & JOLLOF

This one of my personal favorites. The jerk flavors actually originated in Spain. It was developed there, and African slaves picked it up and took it to the Caribbean during the slave trade. It varies slightly from island to island. In Trinidad you will find it very moist and with a strong BBQ influence, in Antigua its really hot, St. Lucians have an added sweetness to it and Jamaicans cook it dry. The word jerk originally means dried strips of meat steaming from jerky. So perhaps the Jamaicans got this one right

TIP: If you have a smoker, smoke it!

Marinade
3 Garlic cloves
1 thumb size piece of ginger (Skin on)
½ bunch of thyme
½ a white onion
2 spring onions
1 scotch bonnet
1 tsp of lemon juice
1 tbsp of honey
1 tbsp of browning
1 tsp of brown sugar
1 tsp of smoked paprika
1 tbsp of all spice
1 tsp of cinnamon
S&P to taste

4 large chicken legs

Start by scoring the skin of the chicken legs 3 slices from the drum through to the thigh. Place all the ingredients in a blender a blitz. Whilst blending add the olive oil until you have a smooth dark brown paste. Pour generously and rub thoroughly into the chicken making sure this is well into the incisions made into the skin and on the bottom of the leg. Cover the chicken in the same bowl with clingfilm and place in the fridge overnight. Before cooking leave the meat at room temperature for 20 minutes to allow it to relax. Add half a cup of boiling water to the baking try before cooking

Place in a pre-heated oven 180°/gas mark 5. For a total of 1 hour. After 30 minutes take the chicken out of the oven and turn over and put back in for the remaining 30 minutes. After 1 hour take it out of the oven and turn it back over. It should now be fully cooked. Turn the oven up to 195°/gas mark 6 and put back in the oven for a further 10 minutes to dry it out.

Serve with Jollof Rice, coleslaw, gravy or BBQ sauce

STEW CHICKEN

SERVES: 4 ≈ COOK: 1.40 HOURS ≈ PREP: 4.5 HOURS

A popular dish among the English-speaking islands in the Caribbean. It is Also known as brown stew chicken because of its dark color. Comforting in smell and addictive in flavor this slow cooked chicken recipe is a table pleaser every time round

TIP: Put all the ingredients in your slow cooker and go to work

4 chicken legs
4 large carrots
3 bell peppers
2 large white onion
½ bunch of thyme
3 spring onions
½ lemon
1 scotch bonnet pierced
4 cloves of garlic
1 thumb size piece of ginger
1 tbsp of browning
1 tbsp of all-purpose seasoning
1 tbsp of smoked paprika
1 tbsp of brown sugar
1 tsp of ketchup
100ml of chicken stock
80ml of water
S&P

Take the chicken and put 3-4 slices in the skin to allow the marinade to sink into the meat.
In a food processor blend together all the ingredients (excluding the stock and water) adding oil until the paste becomes smooth and runny. Cover and marinate for 4 hour or ideally overnight.
Before cooking leave the meat at room temperature for 20 minutes allowing it to relax

Heat a saucepan with oil and brown the chicken on both sides on a medium heat. Once colored add the remaining ingredients adding the water and stock last.

Cover and simmer on a low heat for 1hour 30 minutes. Until the meat is staring to separate from the bone. Make sure you stir regularly.

Remove from the pan and serve with rice and peas and a roti bread

DA GENERALS SANDWICH

SERVES: 2 ≈ COOK: 20 MINUTES HOURS ≈ PREP: 15 MINUTES

The Jerk Burger. I used to ask the staff in the Caribbean take away to put together this burger for me more or less on a daily basis when I was working in the area. He would say "get di general his sandwich". It was messy but I would eat it on the bus with no worries. I recreated it slightly and put it on the menu at our restaurant in Cheam

TIP: Shred and put it in a wrap if you're feeling healthy.

Jerk Paste
1 Garlic clove
½ bunch of thyme
½ a white onion
2 spring onions
1 red chili
1 tbsp of honey
2 tbsp of soy sauce
½ the juice of a lemon
1 tbsp of browning
1 tsp of brown sugar
1 tsp of smoked paprika
1 tsp of all spice
1 tsp of cinnamon
S&P

2 Burger buns
2 Boneless skin on chicken thighs
1 Avocado
BBQ sauce

Slaw
Handful of grated carrot, handful finely sliced red cabbage, 1 tsp of sugar, kewpie mayonnaise

Excluding the soy sauce, honey and browning add all the jerk paste ingredients to a blender and blend until all incorporated. Then slowly add the honey, browning and soy sauce.

Then take your paste and cover the chicken thighs in it. Cover and leave in the fridge for 30 minutes. Whilst chilling start making the slaw. Mix all the ingredients together and place on the bottom of the bun. Take your marinated chicken form the fridge and leave at room temperature for 10 minutes. Heat a heavy base frying pan (Medium heat) with a drizzle of oil and fry skin side down. Once brown turn over and brown the other side. Place the pan in a pre-heated oven 195°/gas mark 5 leave the chicken to finish cooking in the oven for a further 20 minutes.
Once cooked place your chicken on top of the slaw top with a couple of slices of avocado and a twist of BBQ sauce

1960 SOMETHING

SERVES: 2 ≈ COOK: 10 MINUTES HOURS ≈ PREP: 15 MINUTES

This is a creole style roti. With 2 different flavor profiles running through it. It is popular item on our takeaway menu at the restaurant. I name it 1960 something to mark the decade my dad immigrated from St. Lucia to England. Incorporating flavors from both islands. A coronation style dressing and sweet and spicy Caribbean seasonings. I imagine a wrap like this would have been great on the journey

Creole Seasoning
1tsp of sweet paprika
1tsp of cayenne pepper
1tsp of onion powder
1tsp of garlic powder
1tsp of white pepper
1tsp of oregano
4 tbsp of coconut milk
S&P

1 chicken breast
Handful of iceberg lettuce
1 spring onion
Handful of sliced red onion
1 roti

Dressing
2 tbsp of mango chutney, 4 tbsp of good quality mayonnaise, 1 tsp of wholegrain mustard (optional) handful of sliced cashew nut halves and sultanas, sea salt, black pepper

Mix the creole seasoning spices together. Slice your chicken breast into thin strips and mix with half of the creole seasoning and fry with oil on a medium heat. Add the remaining seasoning once brown and fry until cooked. Then add the cashew nuts and sultanas and stir in.

Turn off the heat and add the mango chutney and mix all together then add the mayonnaise, mustard salt and pepper.

Place in your roti with the lettuce, red onion and enjoy.

THAI CHICKEN SATAY

SERVES: 4 ≈ COOK: 35 MINUTES HOURS ≈ PREP: 15 MINUTES

This recipe was invented for a birthday party I did at a golf club I was managing at the time. They were heavily influenced by Thai dishes and we did a full hot and cold Thai buffet. To save room I ended up putting the rice, chicken and pak choi in 1 gastro tin and it looked incredible

200g of crunchy peanut butter
1 tbsp of dark soy sauce
2 tbsp of sweet chili sauce
4 tbsp of rich coconut milk
1 red chili
1tsp of tamarind
2 garlic cloves
1 thumb of galangal or ginger
Half a finely sliced shallot
20 grams of palm or brown sugar
Sea salt

4 boneless skin on chicken thighs
2 pak choi heads

In a food processor blend all the sauce ingredients adding the coconut milk last and some oil towards the end to make it smoother.
Seal the chicken breast in a hot pan on both sides. Skin side first. When brown cover generously in most of the satay sauce. Place in a pre-heated oven at 180°/ gas mark 4 for 20 minutes. Whilst cooking separate your pak choi leaves from the stalk and cook in boiling water for 3 minutes. Take your chicken breasts from the oven drizzle with the remaining satay sauce and garnish with coriander leaves.

Serve with coconut rice and the pak choi

MOK HOI SATAY

SERVES: 2 ≈ COOK: 10 MINUTES ≈ PREP: 10 MINUTES

This is a version of satay chicken usually found in the capital of Hong Kong. Cooked on the streets to order it is fresh, crisp, clean and packed full of flavor

Sauce
200g of crunchy peanut butter
1 tbsp of dark soy sauce
2 tbsp of sweet chili sauce
1 red chili
1tsp of tamarind
2 garlic cloves
1 tbsp of honey
Finley sliced coriander stalks
Sea salt
Vegetable oil
Dry Coating
1 cup of corn flour
2 tbsp of salt
1 tbsp of black pepper
1 tsp of sugar
1 tsp of Chinese 5 spice
1 tsp of chili powder
Wet Coating
2 eggs
100ml of coconut milk

200grams of diced chicken thigh

Mix all the sauce ingredients together in a blender and blend until smooth adding oil as you go. Then set to one side. Mix together all the dry coating making sure it is all thoroughly mixed and set to one side. Mix together the wet coating in a separate bowl and set to one side. Pre heat a pan of rapeseed oil to 165° DON'T take your eyes off it until cooled. It can be really volatile. Always apply caution when deep frying at home. Or ideally us a fat fryer.

Roll your chicken in the wet mix then into the dry mix. Then back into the wet mix and back into the dry mix (note this bit is easier with 2 people) then drop in the hot oil stir it with a dry slotted spoon. Cook for around 8 minutes remove and set to one side, turn your oil off straight away and dispose of in a outside drain. In a hot wok add the blended satay sauce heat and add the chicken. Toss thoroughly and serve with coconut rice.

KING OF SEOUL WINGS

SERVES: 4 ≈ COOK: 10 MINUTES ≈ PREP: 10 MINUTES

1kg buffalo chicken wings
500ml butter milk
2 eggs
3 tbsp Korean red pepper powder
1 tbsp of garlic powder
1 tbsp of ground coriander
1tbsp of salt
2 cups of plain flour
1 cup of corn flour
4 tbsp of light soy sauce
350ml of corn syrup (or make a strong sugar syrup)
1 tsp of sesame oil
2 tsp of Honey
2 tbsp of Gochujang red pepper paste
Juice of 1 lime
Sprinkle of sesame seeds
Coriander leaves

Start by covering the chicken wings in butter milk and mixing thoroughly. Wisk together the eggs and mix in with the wings and butter milk. Also, a pinch of salt. Cover with cling film and leave in the fridge at least 4 hours but ideally overnight.

In a large bowl mix together the flour, corn flour, Korean red pepper powder, garlic powder, ground coriander and salt. Remove the chicken wings from the buttermilk and egg mix. Then roll the chicken wings in the flour mix until thoroughly covered all over. Ensuring all areas are covered in the seasoned flour. Per heat a deep fat fryer to 165° and slowly dip into the hot oil top first until fully submerged, repeat this process with each wing.

Allow 8-10 minutes of cooking time. Ideally use a temperature probe and poke the fleshy part of the chicken. Making sure the thermometer is not quite touching the bone. It should read 75 degrees + and outer layer should be crispy and a golden color. Pull out and leave on a wire rack and cover in foil to keep warm.

Then make the sauce. Heat in a small saucepan. Corn syrup, soy sauce, sesame oil and honey and thoroughly mix. Once warm and the juice of half a lime and mix again. Then add the gochujang paste and mix until it is a vibrant red color. Remove from the heat then dip the warm wings in the sauce so they are fully submerged remove from the sauce and plate up.

You can make this sauce in advance and keep refrigerated.

Garnish with half a grilled lime, sesame seeds and coriander leaves.

MALAY 48

SERVES: 2 ≈ COOK: 10 MINUTES ≈ PREP: 15 MINUTES

Part of our company is our brand and restaurant "Uptown Flava". So, it wouldn't be right if I dropped this book and didn't drop our most popular recipe. I had to leave out 2 ingredients but hay this should do the job

8 chicken fillet strips or tenders
Wet Mix
500ml of butter milk
1 egg
2 egg yokes

Rapeseed oil for deep frying
Dry Mix
1 cup of corn flour
1 cup of plain flour
1 tbsp of smoked paprika
1 tbsp of dried marjoram
1 tbsp of onion powder
1 tbsp of garlic flour
1 tbsp of mustard powder
1 tsp of celery salt
1 tbsp of caster sugar
2 tbsp of all-purpose seasoning
1 tbsp of salt
1tbsp of sea salt
1 tbsp of white pepper
Sauce
5 tbsp of corn syrup, 2 tbsp of sweet chili sauce 1 tbsp of light soy sauce 1tsb of honey 1tsp finely chopped coriander stalks.

Mix together the wet mix in one bowl and the dry mix in another. Add half of the dry spice mix to the butter milk and mix. Then add the chicken the butter milk mix. Make sure it is fully submerged or sealed. Leave in the fridge for 4 hours. Whilst marinating mix all the sauce ingredients in a saucepan and gently heat it together. Once combined move from the heat and set to one side. Mix the remaining dry spice mix into the flours.

Take your chicken out of the fridge and leave at room temperature for half and hour. Heat the oil to 158° Roll the marinated chicken in the flour mix once and fry for around 7 minutes depending on the size of the goujons. Once cooked place to one side and safely dispose of the hot vegetable oil. Re heat the sauce until it looks sticky around the edges add the chicken to it and serve with kewpie mayonnaise and garnish with sesame seeds, spring onion and coriander.

THE UPTOWN GIRL

SERVES: 2 ≈ COOK: 10 MINUTES ≈ PREP: 15 MINUTES

This is one of our 4 staple burgers from the "Uptown Flava" restaurant really simple and straight forward crunchy on the outside moist in then center and stunning to look at.

2 Boneless chicken thighs (Skin off)
Wet Mix
500ml of butter milk
1 egg
2 egg yokes
Rapeseed oil for deep frying
Dry Mix
1 tbsp of smoked paprika
1 tbsp of dried oregano
1 tbsp of onion powder
1 tbsp of garlic flour
1 tbsp of mustard powder
1 tsp of celery salt
1 tbsp of caster sugar
2 tbsp of Cajun seasoning
1 tsp of baking powder
1 tbsp of salt
1 tbsp of white pepper

1 cup of corn flour
1 cup of plain flour

2 burger buns, shredded iceberg lettuce, 2 slices of beef tomato, 4 tablespoons of chili jam 2 tablespoons of kewpie mayonnaise

Mix together the wet mix in one bowl and the dry mix in another. Add half of the dry spice mix to the butter milk and mix. Then add the chicken the butter milk mix. Make sure it is fully submerged or sealed. Leave in the fridge for 4 hours. Whilst marinating mix the remaining dry spice mix into the flours.

Take your chicken out of the fridge and leave at room temperature for half an hour. Heat a deep saucepan with oil to 160°. Roll the marinated chicken in the flour mix once and fry for around 10 minutes depending on the size of the thighs. Once cooked place to one side and safely dispose of the hot vegetable oil. Slice and toast your burger buns and place the chili jam on the bottom and the lettuce and tomato on top of the jam and a good squirt of kewpie mayonnaise to the top of the bun place the chicken in between and munch.

TANDOORI TIKKA MASALA

SERVES: 2 ≈ COOK: 30 MINUTES ≈ PREP: 15 MINUTES

I have been cooking this one for years now. Mainly at curry nights and groups social events. It's an all-round curry with some of the flavors of a tikka masala but with a bit more bite.

500grams diced chicken breast
Half a cup of ghee or vegetable oil
3 large Spanish onions
Finley sliced coriander stalks
5-8 cloves
5 large garlic cloves
100g fresh ginger
4 tbsp of coconut powder
3 tbsp of ground almonds
1 tbsp of caster sugar
2 tbsp of smoked paprika
2 tbsp of dry tandoori seasoning
1 tbsp of gram masala
1 tbsp of tomato pure
Half a tin of full fat coconut milk

0.5 pint of double cream
1 cup of chicken stock or curry sauce
200ml of natural yogurt

Mix your diced chicken with 1 tbsp of smoked paprika and 1 tbsp of tandoori masala and a pinch of salt. Rub together thoroughly until deep red Leave in the fridge overnight. Once marinated splash with vegetable oil and place in the oven at 190°/gas mark 5. Leave for 20-25 minutes (until fully cooked) In a large heavy based pan heat ghee until boiling hot. Then add your cloves to the hot oil after 60 second tip the pan to an angle and remove the cloves from the oil using a large spoon or small sieve. Then return to the heat and add your onions. Leave on a low heat to slightly caramelized.

Then add your garlic and ginger to a robot coup and blend. (Make sure your ginger and garlic are both pealed to save time you can make this in advance) you may need to add a couple splashes of water during this process to help it mix thoroughly. Then add the very finely sliced coriander stalks
Once blended add to the softened onions and stir. Then add your coconut powder, ground almonds and 1 tbsp of tandoori masala and 1 tbsp of gram masala.
Then add 1 tbsp of tomato puree, and one-half tin of full fat coconut milk and 1 tbsp of caster sugar.
Continue to mix on a low heat. After 4-6 minutes remove the chicken from the oven and add to the mix (Include any fat that has come out of the chicken) mix together thoroughly.
Then add your chicken stock or curry base sauce. Allow to simmer for a further 8-10 minutes. To thicken

then add the natural yogurt stir for 30 seconds add the double cream and remove from the heat and share.

SPANISH CHICKEN

SERVES: 4 ≈ COOK: 20 MINUTES ≈ PREP: 10 MINUTES

I use this recipe at home from time to time. It is easy to vary if you are short on time or don't have all the
ingredients. Either way its super tasty and great for the children

500g of diced chicken breast
100g of hot raw chorizo stick
2 red bell peppers
1 large potato
2 shallots
1 tbsp of garlic puree

3 tbsp of smoked paprika
1 tbsp of sweet paprika
1 tsp of oregano
1 tsp of cayenne pepper
Sea salt flakes

Handful of flatleaf parsley
Sprigs of Saffron
800g of chopped tomato
Black pepper

Pre boil the chorizo until cooked and retain the cooking liquid. Slice the cooked chorizo into bite size chunks and
expect it to crumble

In a large frying pan heat olive oil and sauté finely sliced shallots until soft then add the diced red pepper.   add the
spice mix and stir. Then add the chorizo and chicken and sauté for 5 minutes. Then add the garlic puree and the
chopped tomatoes and simmer for 15 minutes stirring regularly. Finally add the salt, pepper, saffron and parsley
mix and simmer for a further 5 minutes. Finish with the retained liquid for the boiled chorizo and a splash of
double cream

Serve with paella rice

SEAFOOD

.

KING PRAWN BEZULE

SERVES: 2 ≈ COOK: 5 MINUTES ≈ PREP: 15 MINUTES

This is a fantastic starter, unique in texture, moreish in taste and stunning in appearance. It originates on the Malabar Coast in south India. The region itself is stunning and still very much in tack from the arrival of the Arabs to Kerala. Another part of the region known for its amazingly unique foods

TIP: this recipe work well with stripped chicken as well

14 Large King Prawns (Raw, Pealed & Deveined)
5 tbsp of vegetable oil
250g of natural yogurt
5 fresh curry leaves
2 tsp of rice flour
1 tbsp of corn flour
1 tbsp of ground cumin
1 tsp of ground ginger
1 tsp of garlic puree
2 tbsp of Kashmiri chilli powder
2 tsp of gram masala
1 tbsp of salt
1 Green chilli (chopped)
1 tbsp of lemon juice
Handful of coriander stalks and leaves
pinch of red food colouring powder

In a food processor place, curry leaves, garlic puree, green chill, and coriander. Blend until course.
Then add to the blender, the rice flour, corn flour, cumin, ginger, chili powder, gram masala, salt and blend again for a further 60 seconds until thoroughly mixed.

Then place lemon juice and the red food coloring and mix in with the natural yogurt. Then fold in the paste from the blender into the yogurt mix.
Once this is thoroughly mixed together place your prawns into the mix, so they are fully covered and place into the fridge for 2-4 hours. (Don't leave for more than this you will find the lemon juice will start to cook the prawns)

Remove from the fridge and leave at room temperature for 20 minutes.

In a wok heat vegetable oil and slowly place your prawns into the hot oil. Cook for 2 minutes on each side. Leave on a wire rack to drain any excess oil and serve with flat bread and mint yogurt or siracha

PRAWNS MANCHURIN

SERVES: 2 ≈ COOK: 5 MINUTES ≈ PREP: 10 MINUTES

This is a really authentic fusion recipe. It was hard to pinpoint but it's believed to have originated in Calcutta from a small Chinese community living there. It's hard to believe but there is a lot of cross over from eastern and western cultures. This is known as Indochinese cuisine or Chadian cuisine

This prawn recipe is a real crowd pleaser totally different from your standard prawn starter recipe. It full of unique flavor from the first bite and hits the taste buds hard with a big hello.

Tip: Place in a paratha wrap

250g Of fresh king prawns
1 Large egg
1 Cup of corn flour
S&P
Vegetable oil

Sauce
2 Cloves of garlic finely chopped
1 inch of fresh ginger
1 green chili finely chopped including seeds
1 red chili finely chopped including seeds
Half a red onion finely diced
1 tbsp of ketchup
1 tbsp of red chili paste
2 tbsp or rich dark soy sauce
1 tbsp of balsamic glaze
Half a cup of cold water
2 spring onions sliced

Take your prawns and toss them in the egg (whisked) corn flour, and salt. Mix thoroughly. Heat vegetable oil in a high rimmed frying pan and deep fray the prawns for 3 minutes until crisp. Allow to drain on a wire rack whilst making the sauce.

In the same pan (oil drained) add garlic, ginger, red onions and chilis and allow to sweat down for 2 minutes. Then add the ketchup, and the chili paste and mix. Then add the soy sauce and mix thoroughly. Finely slowly add the water mix again and leave to reduce on a medium heat until thick about 8 minutes depending on the pan

Once thickened add the precooked prawns to the pan and toss thoroughly leave on the heat for one minute and serve garnish with the spring onion.

KKPAUNG (KOREAN PRAWNS)

SERVES: 2 ≈ COOK: 5 MINUTES ≈ PREP: 15 MINUTES

I'm a personal fan of this recipe. It originated on the streets of Korea where they are famous for fried foods tossed in moreish sauces. Strong, bold, distinctive, flavors dominate Korean cuisine and are evident in this recipe. If you understand food, you know when you bite into a Korean dish. These prawns only confirm that.

TIP: You can Eat cold the following day

10-12 King prawns (raw peeled and deveined)
2 cups of vegetable oil
2 tbsp of potato starch
2 large egg
1 tbsp of sea salt
1 tbsp of ground black pepper
1 tbsp on light soy sauce
1 tbsp of mirin
2 tbsp of Goujon red pepper paste
1 tbsp of oyster sauce
2 tbsp of caster sugar
1 tbsp of rice vinegar
1 tbsp of sesame oil
2 Peeled garlic cloves finely sliced
10g of ginger peeled
1 green pepper finely diced
1 spring onion finely sliced

Whisk you eggs together and dip your prawns into the egg. If your prawns are frozen allow enough time to thoroughly thaw and defrost. Make sure they are dry before dipping into the egg mix.

Mix your potato starch, salt and pepper together thoroughly. Roll your prawns through the mix. Heat up your vegetable oil in a heavy based sauté' pan. Once piping hot add your prawns 1 at a time so they are flat in the pan. No more than 1 minute on each side.

Once they are cooked remove and leave on a wire tray and add the aromatic mix to the same oil.

Whilst they are cooking whisk all the sauce ingredients together in a large bowl until thoroughly mixed and add the part cooked vegetables. Then return the prawns to the pan so submerged in the oil.

Remove with a slotted spoon leaving any excess mix. Garnish coriander leaves and enjoy

THAI SATAY PRAWNS

SERVES: 2 ≈ COOK: 5 MINUTES ≈ PREP: 10 MINUTES

You will find these prawns in most restaurants in Thailand. Some of the coastal regions catch these fresh and cook soon after. It's really quick and easy to do. This satay sauce is lighter and more fish friendly. It cooks out really thick and works great with coconut rice

TIP: Served with naan instead of rice

150grams of smooth peanut butter
2 tbsp of dark soy sauce
1 tbsp of honey
Juice of half a lemon
1 tbsp of fish sauce
1 green chili
½ bunch of coriander
2 sticks of lemon grass
1 red pepper (Diced)
100g of mange toot
400ml of coconut milk
2 kaffir lime leaves

In a food processor add all the satay sauce ingredients and blitz expect it to be course it will break down once heated with the coconut milk.

In a large frying pan or wok. Sauté the sugar snap peas, lemongrass and red peppers. After 3-4 minutes add the prawns and toss regularly for 2 minutes. Then the kaffir lime leaves. Then the satay paste. Slowly add coconut milk and stir it in until you have a smooth sauce.

 Leave to simmer for 2 further minutes

And share.

SINGAPOUR CRACKED CRAB

SERVES: 1 ≈ COOK: 5 MINUTES ≈ PREP: 20 MINUTES

When eating this dish, you must be prepared to get a bit messy no matter how well you use a crustacean cracker you will need your hands for this one.

The Weston culture is still amazed to this day to see people eating this on the streets of Singapore. I don't blame them the flavors are on point. Not to overpowering for the delicate crab as it is cooked in the shell it still retains a lot of the gentle flavors.

TIP: Use a nutcracker for the claws

1 whole crab (Cooked)
4 tbsp of vegetable oil
1 Red chill sliced
1 green chilli sliced
2 cloves of garlic finely sliced length ways
Thumb size piece of ginger cut into matchsticks
2 spring onions finely sliced diagonally
Handful of coriander leaves picked
3 tbsp of ketchup
3 tbsp of dark soy sauce
Sprinkle of sesame seeds

Ask you fish monger to prep your crab before use. It will need to be fully cooked, dead man's fingers removed and the claws and legs have been cracked slightly this allows the sauce to get into the meat.

Heat the oil in a wok until boiling hot add the chilli garlic, ginger and spring onions. Stir until soft about 1 minute then add the ketchup and soy sauce and mix all together.

Add the crab to the hot pan and keep mixing in until it is all thoroughly covered in the sauce keep stirring for about 5 minutes on a high heat.

Then remove for the pan with a long pair of tongs or serving spoon and retain most the sauce garnish with coriander leaves and sesame seeds.

LOBSTER MAC & CHEESE

SERVES: 2 ≈ COOK: 25 MINUTES ≈ PREP: 15 MINUTES

You can't help but love this recipe it is a bit labour intensive especially if you have to cook your lobster from fresh. But it dose consists of some great flavours. If you like fish and you saw this on a menu you would have to buy it just because.

TIP: Mix the parmesan with panko breadcrumbs before baking

200g lobster meat

100g of gruyere cheese
50g of plain flour
1 leek very finely sliced
1 shallot finely sliced
200ml of double cream
400ml of whole milk
60grams of salted butter
1 bay leaf
Sea salt
Pepper
100g of macaroni pasta

Start by boiling your macaroni pasta in salted water. I always over cook macaroni pasta I find it makes better for a soft macaroni bake. Once cooked strain the hot water but don't cool it down. Leave it in the residual heat.

Then on to the cheese sauce. Add the butter and melt then the shallot, leek and the bay leaf. Once soft add the flour and stir. Slowly add the hot milk and stir into the roux as. Once you have used the milk slowly fold in the cold cream. Don't worry if it is to runny the cheese will thicken it up. Keep the sauce on a low heat and add the cheese stir after one-minute remove from the heat and gently fold in the lobster meat to the sauce. Pour generously over the macaroni pasta making sure it is tightly packed in your baking dish. Top with a dusting of parmesan cheese and bake for 12 minutes at 175° / gas mark 3. Enjoy

SALT FISH FRITTERS & MANGO SALAD

SERVES: 2 ≈ COOK: 10 MINUTES ≈ PREP: 3 HOURS

The catering industry is as competitive as it gets everyone's recipe is better than the next chefs. It's difficult for me to admit that my cousin's recipe for these fritters is better than mine. She first introduced me to this salty snack and up until recently I haven't attempted to recreate them. So, this recipe below is hers, with a few of my twists.

300g Of Salted Cod
Half a large onion finely chopped
2 spring onions (very finely chopped)
Half a sweet red pepper
2 red chillies finely chopped (deseeded)
1 egg
1 tbsp of cracked black pepper
1 tbsp of sea salt
1 tsp of lemon juice
750ml of vegetable oil

1 ripe mango
Half a diced red onion
Handful of picked coriander leaves
1 tbsp of sweetcorn

TIP: Pour boiling water over the salt cod to save time

Place the salted cod in a colander and run the cold tap over it and leave running for 20 minutes. Then turn it over and let the water run on the other side.
Then place in a bowl of cold water for 2 hours in the fridge. Change the water over after 1 hour and place back in the fridge for the last hour.
Whilst this is soaking finely dice your peppers, onions, and chili and mix together with the seasoning, then add the lemon juice mix again. Wisk your egg in a separate bowl and add to the mix.
Then remove you cod from the water and shake above the sink. Flake with a fork into the mix and mix. Sift in the flour and stir again
Heat the oil in a saucepan. Heat till about 170°
Then take a spoon of the mix and drop it into the hot oil 1 at a time until each one is golden brown. Roughly 2 minutes then leave on a wire rack or kitchen towel.

Take your mango and cut it into bite size chunks. Place in a bowl, add your red onion, sweet corn lime juice, sugar and coriander leaves. Place on your plate and enjoy

CRAB CAKES

SERVES: 2 ≈ COOK: 8 MINUTES ≈ PREP: 15 MINUTES

I created this recipe after going through a phase of eating fish cakes. I was over frozen prawn cakes from the supermarket. So, I used fresh fish and added the sweetness with a chili jam. And this recipe is partially on point

TIP: If you alter the fish use a light shellfish and an oily one for a balanced texture

100g of white crab meat
100g of fresh salmon (Skinned)
25g of Fresh Ginger
Handful of coriander leaves
1 garlic clove
1 Stick of Lemon Grass
1 Lime
1 Red Chill Deseeded and Finley Chopped
1 tsp of honey
Handful of panko breadcrumbs
2 eggs
2 tbsp of whole milk

First place your salmon in a shallow tray and into the oven half submerged in hot water. (Chuck a bay leaf in for good measure) cook at 170° / gas mark 4 for 8 minutes then allow to cool and flake into a bowl.

Fold in with the crab meat gently.

In a blender add ginger lemon grass (finely chopped chop off the rough green end and discard). Add the juice and zest on 1 whole lime. Whole red chill (No Seeds) 1 garlic clove & 1 tsp of honey. Then blend using the pulse button on the blender. For 40 seconds on and off and mix back together from time to time.

Add a pinch of salt and fold again.

Then roll in your hands into 1-2-inch balls and flatten with your hands. After rolling for about 40 seconds you can then start pushing down on them to form the cake roughly 2 centimetres but is personal preference.

Once made mix together the egg and the milk in a separate bowl and run the fish cake through it and then mix through the panko breadcrumbs. Drizzle lightly with olive oil and place in a pre-heated oven on 190° / gas mark 6 for 15-18 minutes and serve with chili jam.

RED SNAPPER IN MISO BROTH

SERVES: 1 ≈ COOK: 15 MINUTES ≈ PREP: 10NMINUTES

This is a strong confident dish. Big bold and beautiful. Also, really inexpensive. If you can keep your freezer loaded up snapper it is a fish that retains flavor well when frozen. Meaty in flavor and delicious. It is really underrated

TIP: Score the fish skin with a sharp knife before rubbing with salt

1 170g red snapper fillet
2 tsp of miso paste
1 large onion finely diced
2 thumbs of grated galangal or ginger
1 tbsp of dark soy sauce
1tbsp of roasted sesame oil
1 bay leaf
1 stick of lemon grass crushed
2 cups of fish stock
1 cup of chicken stock
Handful of rice noodles
Handful of bean sprouts
Salt

To a hot pan add oil and sweat off the diced onion, galangal and the bay leaf. Add 2 cups of fish stock, and bring to the boil, add the miso paste and the lemon grass and turn down to simmer.

Then add the rice noodles and bean sprouts and leave for 10 minutes. The add the soy sauce and sesame oil and stir. Finally drop in the red snapper and salt (top up with water if needed) cover and leave to cook for 10 minutes. Ladled our carefully and enjoy.

MEAT

LAMB KORAI

SERVES: 2 ≈ COOK: 1 HOUR ≈ PREP: 15 MINUTES

This is my favourite lamb curry recipe. My regular go to when I am in an authentic Indian restaurant. I have adjusted it a bit and making it slightly thicker and added a little extra spice

TIP: Leave in the fridge over night after making and the flavour will intensify

500g of diced lamb neck fillet
4 tbsp of Ghee (Or Vegetable Oil)
4 garlic cloves finely sliced
2 tbsp of garlic and ginger puree
8 fresh tomatoes (Skinned and chopped sliced)
3 large onions (Chunky Dice)
2 tbsp of Kashmiri chilli powder
1 tbsp of ground coriander
1 tbsp of ground cumin
1 tsp of ground turmeric
1 tsp of tandoori seasoning
1 tbsp of cumin seeds
1 tbsp of garam masala powder
1 tablespoon of salt
10 fresh curry leaves
2 tbsp of salt
2 green chili (deseeded and finely sliced)
1 red chilli opened down the middle
Handful of chopped coriander leaves
4 tbsp of natural yogurt
400ml of coconut milk
1 tbsp of double cream

Add diced lamb to a mixing bowl mix in 2 tbsp of natural yogurt, 1 tbsp of ground cumin, 1 tsp of tandoori seasoning, mix cover in cling film and leave in the fridge overnight. (Leave the lamb at room temperature for 30 minutes before cooking)

Heat your ghee or vegetable oil in a heavy based saucepan. Once hot add your onions roughly chopped and stir until soft and start to turn brown. Add splashes of water to stop from burning Then add the remaining spices. Stir in and leave to cook out for 3-4 minutes adding splashed of water where needed. Then turn down the heat. Add the lamb in batches including the marinade and brown. thoroughly (stir constantly and keep the heat low so the marinade doesn't split)

Then add the tomatoes and stir together. Then add the coconut milk (you may need to add more whilst it is simmering) you want the end result to be thick. Throw in your red chili still connected by the stalk so it can be easily removed.

And leave to simmer for 45-55 minutes stirring regularly

NORTH AFRICAN PULLED LAMB

SERVES: 6 ≈ COOK: 5 HOURS ≈ PREP: 15 MINUTES

This dish takes 6 hours or so but is so worth it. If you have a clear Sunday morning and have the time to invest in a dinner, then this is the way forward. You will find it tender and tasty and you will enjoy the leftovers on Monday morning. Originally it is from north Africa it is eaten a lot with lentils. This one calls for couscous but if you prefer lentils or rice than it works well with both

2.5kg Lamb Shoulder
1 large lemon roughly sliced
2 large onions
1 bunch of rosemary
1 bunch of thyme
2 red chilis

Marinade
2 tbsp of tahini
1 tbsp of harissa
1 tbsp of ground cinnamon
2 tbsp of ground cumin
1 tsp of ground coriander
1 tsp of cayenne pepper
1 tsp of garlic and ginger paste
1 tbsp of honey
2 tbsp of melted and chilled butter
1 tbsp on olive oil

Place your lamb shoulder on baking tray make 4-5 2cm, slices in the lamb skin about 2 millimeters deep until the tip of your knife hits the bottom of the fat. In a large mixing bowl mix together all your marinade ingredients. Then pour over the lamb and into the incisions. Cover in cling film and leave in the fridge overnight.

Remove the lamb and leave at room temperature for 30 minutes. Pour 2 cups of water into the bottom of the oven tray. Roughly slice the onion, lemon and place in the water in the tray. Also, ½ a bunch of rosemary and ½ bunch of thyme. Cover your lamb with strips of foil making sure it is covered fully with no gaps.

Place in a pre-heated oven to 160° / gas mark 3 and cook for 3 hours. And baste with the juices every hour. Remove the lamb from the oven and place upside down in the tray only one layer of foil on top fully covered and place back in the oven for 1 hour. For the final hour remove the lamb from the oven turn back up the other way sprinkle thoroughly with the gram masala and turn the heat up to 190° / gas mark 5 and place the lamb back in the oven with no foil.

Then remove your lamb from the oven and leave to rest for 15 minutes

Place your flat breads on your plate, 2 tbsp of couscous. as much shredded lamb as you can manage. Add a small pot of sour cream and garnish with crushed pistachio nuts. Save any lamb for the following days. Works great in a wrap or salad.

HARRISA LAMB BURGERS

SERVES: 2 ≈ COOK: 20 MINUTES ≈ PREP: 10 MINUTES

This is one really is one from the person scrap book that I keep in my back pocket. Like most of you would agree you can't beat a good burger and at the moment there are so many variations and ways to do them. I have always preferred lamb over beef and the flavours below bring real flavour whilst still preserving the taste of lamb

TIP: Top with tzatziki and couscous if you want to pimp it out a little

400g of lean lamb mince
2 tbsp of Moroccan seasoning
2 tbsp of ground cumin
1tsp of ground coriander
1 tsp of cayenne pepper
1tbsp of sweet paprika
1 tbsp of cooking salt
1 tsp of harissa paste
1 tsp of tahini
Handful of fresh mint leaves very finely sliced
2 large eggs (Pre-whisked)
S&P

2 crusty ciabattas
2 handfuls of water cress
4 tbsp of mint yogurt
Sliced halloumi

In a wide rimed mixing bowl place, the lamb mince, salt and mix. Then add the Moroccan seasoning, cumin. cayenne pepper, coriander, paprika, harissa paste, tahini and fresh mint. The mix together thoroughly (be rough as you can so you push the seasoning into the mice) the longer you mix the better.

Then add the mix leaves and eggs and mix again for 1 minute.

Fold into balls. Then mold with your hand into burgers. Start with a large meat ball and keep rolling once you have a solid feel push down until roughly 1 cm flat.

Cover in cling film and leave in the fridge for 2 hours.
Heat a griddle pan until smokey and place your burger in the pan for 2 minutes on each side. Finish in a preheated oven at 180°/ gas mark 4 for 10 minutes. If you have probe 60 degrees is good with lean lamb mince.
Whilst cooking rub 2 tablespoon of vegetable oil into the ciabatta and place under the grill only toast the inside. Generously rub the mint yogurt into the top of the ciabatta and place the watercress on the bottom.

When ready place the burger in the ciabatta and tuck in

LAMB TAGINE

SERVES: 2 ≈ COOK: 2.5 HOUR ≈ PREP: OVERNIGHT

Got to love a tagine and with my addiction to Moroccan food growing by the day I had to create a puka tagine recipe.
This one gives you a great balance of sweetness and spice
Really is like sitting a crowded market in morocco absorbing all the climate.
(add a backdrop to your kitchen for the complete experience)
This recipe doesn't call to a tagine pot as I think they only work in areas indigenous to the pot and require stone clay ovens (in my opinion) the recipe I am sharing with you below gives you all the authentic tastes of morocco using classic cookery methods

480 grams of diced lamb shoulder
Marinade
3 tbsp of tahini, 1 tsp of ras el hanout, 1 tbsp of ground turmeric, 2 tbsp of ground cumin, 1 tbsp of manuka honey, 1 tbsp of salt
Sauce
1 large onion roughly sliced
800g of chopped tomatoes
1 tbsp of ground cinnamon
1 tbsp of ras el hanout
1 tbsp of salt
1 tbsp of ground cumin
2 tbsp of plain flour
1 tbsp of tomato puree
1 tsp of ground turmeric
1 tsp of ground coriander
1 tsp sweet paprika
1 tbsp of natural yogurt
1 tsp of garlic and ginger puree
1 cup of lamb or chicken stock
1 cinnamon stick
2 bay leaves
Half a lemon finely sliced
100g of chopped apricots
50g of toasted almonds
Handful of pomegranate seeds

Mix together tahini, the ras el hanout, cumin, honey and salt. Spend some time rubbing it into the lamb cover it completely. Cover in cling film and place in the fridge overnight.
Once marinated seal the lamb in a large pan brushed with oil. Once brown all over remove and leave to one side at room temperature Heat oil in a large saucepan add the onion. Once soft add the garlic and ginger puree. Cook for 1 minute then add the ground cinnamon, cumin, turmeric, paprika, coriander, flour and tomato puree and stir together cook for 3-4 minutes then add the chopped tomatoes, lemon slices, stock and the diced lamb stir all together. Cover and simmer for 1 hour and a half until the lamb is soft and tender. In the last-minute mix in the yogurt
Place the sliced almonds on a lined tray and under the grill on a low heat until brown mix with the pomegranate seeds and sprinkle on top of the tagine

LAMB SHANK MASSAMAM

SERVES: 2 ≈ COOK: 3 HOURS ≈ PREP: 10 MINUTES

We all love a massamam curry rich in Thai flavor and comforting to taste. The question is do you serve it with rice? or is the potato enough

2 Lamb Shanks
2 larger waxy potatoes
8 sticks of lemon grass (chopped)
3 inches of galangal or fresh ginger
60gs of dried red chilis (No seeds)
6 cloves of garlic
Handful of sliced coriander stalks
100g or roasted peanuts
1 tbsp of ground nutmeg
2 tbsp of cumin
Handful of mace sheathes

2 cinnamon sticks
800g of coconut milk

Add all the paste items to a food processor and blend. Ideally put the whole items through a pestle mortar first to release the flavors. Once made keep the paste at room temperature if you are using it straight away

In a warm saucepan add the massamam paste and slowly add the tamarind once incorporated add the coconut milk and simmer for 5 minutes. Take half of the liquid and pour it over the lamb shanks and place them in a pre heated oven on 160° / gas mark 5 it needs to be in the oven for around 3 hours and turned over every hour with more sauce added to it every hour until it has all been used up. For the last 10 minutes turn the heat up to 190° gas mark 5.

It's now ready the choice of the added rice is up to you

CURRY GOAT

SERVES: 2 ≈ COOK: 4 HOURS ≈ PREP: 20 MINUTES

This recipe takes me back to my auntie's home. With all the family gathered around enjoying stories and great memories. The curry goat was always the firsts to go. Wherever I am whenever I eat it, I think of her and the fun we had around the dinner table enjoying her food. I can proudly say her goat curry beats mine, hands down. That being said my recipe is pretty hot. Cook this one and feel the flavour.

TIP: Use a good quality Jamaican curry powder

500g Diced Goat Meat (can be substituted with mutton)

1 large onion chunky dice
3 spring onions roughly chopped
6 sprigs of fresh thyme
3 waxy potatoes (Cut into thick chunks)
1 scotch bonnet pepper with (3 small piercings)
2 tbsp of tomato puree
2 tbsp of garlic and ginger puree
1 tbsp of ground turmeric
1 tbsp of natural yogurt
3 tbsp of curry powder (Jamaican)
450ml of chicken stock
2 tsp of salt

Marinate the goat meat for 4 hours or ideally overnight. Mix into it half the curry powder, turmeric, garlic and ginger puree, and salt. Cover in cling film and place in the fridge.

Once marinated. Heat a splash of oil in a frying pan and seal the goat meat until brown all over. Do this in batches. Once sealed place in a casserole dish (don't leave any of the marinade in the bowl make sure it all ends up in the casserole dish)
Then in the same pan brown the onion and thyme. Once softened add the tomato puree the remaining curry powder and mix together until all fully incorporated and add the casserole dish.
Add the stock a twist more of salt and the pierced scotch bonnet stir and leave to simmer for slowly for 2.5-3 hours. Whilst cooking cut and peal your potatoes into cubes in a place in the curry for the last 45 minutes Once cooked leave to chill then add the stew

Check meat is tender once soft remove from the heat stir in the natural yogurt. Mix thoroughly and serve with rice and peas

BEEF CHILI AND SWEET POTAT0 CRISPS

SERVES: 4 ≈ COOK: 4 HOURS ≈ PREP: 20 MINUTES

This is a real foodie delight current meets classic. Great for social events and eating on the street out a box with a plastic fork. Chili really has stood the test of time packed full of various flavors and so versatile. For me you need lots of deep red smoked paprika and chili. I can't stand a bland chili it's in the title CHILI it is meant to have kick and lots of sweet tomato running through it.

This recipe has exactly that I love serving this on my street food trailer with lots of sour cream, guacamole, siracha and chives and topped with the sauté sweet potato slices. Always sells out every time

1kg of lean beef mince
200g of kidney beans
150g of mixed diced pepper
150ml of beef stock

4 tbsp of tomato puree
400g of chopped tomatoes
5 garlic cloves grated
1 tbsp of Worcester sauce
1 large Spanish onion roughly diced
1 tbsp of cayenne pepper
1 tsp of chili powder
2 tbsp of smoked paprika
1 tbsp of ground coriander
1 tbsp of ground cumin
1 tbsp cooking salt
1 tsp of sea salt
3 tbsp of sour cream
1 large sweet potato sliced.

In a heavy based pan heat vegetable oil on a low heat. Add the onion and garlic and soften together for 3-4 minutes. The add the mixed peppers and half of the salt and stir. Leave to soften for a further 4 minutes on a medium heat.

Then add the beef mice turn the heat up a stir in until the mince is brown all over. Add the tomato puree, paprika, cumin, coriander, chili powder, cayenne pepper and stir all together. Add the beef stock and chopped tomatoes mix back together and leave to simmer for 50minutes. Stirring occasionally.

Then crack on with the sweet potato crisps.

Peal a whole sweet potato and finely slice it into round 2ml discs. Aim to get these as thin as possible to decrease the cooking time.

Once sliced in a separate pan heat 10 tablespoons of vegetable oil. Keep on a low heat. Place the slices of sweet potato in and cook for 1 minute and a half on each side. The place and a wire rack and sprinkle with sea salt.

Once 50 minutes has passed add the remaining salt to the chili con carne. Stir and leave for a furthers 5 minutes. Top with sour cream and harissa

STREET FOOD AND SPICE

KEITHS BEEF STROGNOFF

SERVES: 4 ≈ COOK: 25 MINUTES ≈ PREP: 10 MINUTES

I first came across this recipe working with a chef named Keith. I was only an apprentice at the time, but you always know good food when you find it. This guy really had his food down. He shared this recipe with me after I kepted badgering him for it. I have since adapted it. Defiantly worth cooking sweet and moreish will fill you up every time.

TIP: Call Keith

500g of stripped beef fillet stroganoff
200ml of dark soy sauce
100ml light soy sauce
50g of caster sugar
50g of soft dark brown sugar
1 tbspof fish sauce
1 tsp of sesame oil
Handful of sesame seeds
Handful of coriander leaves
Handful of toasted cashew nuts
1 tbsp of sea salt

In a heavy based saucepan add 500ml of boiling water. Once the water is boiling away add the sugar after 2 minutes turn the heat down and allow to dissolve. After 5 minutes you should have the base of your sugar syrup. Then add the soy sauce and stir remove from the heat and allow to cool.

Then in a hot wok add oil then your beef toss and stir for 5 minutes until sealed add the salt, fish sauce and sesame oil continue to fry the beef for a further 3-4 minutes. Then add to the saucepan with the sugar syrup add all juices for the beef as well. leave on a low heat for 4 minutes.

Then brown your cashew nuts in the same wok you cooked the beef in.

Remove beef from the saucepan with a slotted spoon and throw over some sticky rice. Garnish with more cashew nuts and coriander leaves

CHORIZO, HALLOUMI BEEF AND SWEET CHILI BURGERS

SERVES: 2 ≈ COOK: 15 MINUTES ≈ PREP: 15 MINUTES

We sell these in the summer at various BBQs and weddings they are always a crowd pleaser. Packed full of flavour and the crunchy sweet chorizo running through it just takes burger patties to another level. I added this to our summer menu in 2014 after doing a Free BBQ at my church. Not having any menu restraints, I was able to adapt my usual recipes and take them up a notch. Whenever you're making burgers to this recipe you won't be disappointed. The secret ingredient believes it or not is ketchup adds a great subtle sweetness without burning.

TIP: Retain all the oil from the pan when you sauté the chorizo that's where all the hidden flavour is

1 Brioche Bun (Ideally Seeded)
500g of lean beef mince
150g of finely diced Spanish chorizo
2 tbsp of smoked paprika
2 tbsp of tomato ketchup
1 tbsp of honey
2 tbsp of Cajun spice
1 large free-range egg
S&P
1 sliced of halloumi
Finley diced red onion
Very finely chopped coriander
Sea salt flakes

In a large mixing bowl add you beef mince break it up slightly. Tablespoon of salt and pepper mixed, Paprika, Cajun spice, honey, ketchup, diced red onion (Pre fried) and very finely sliced coriander mix together thoroughly.

In a pan add a splash of oil and cook your chorizo for 8-10 minutes until brown and all the juice has escaped.

Then add the chorizo to the burger mix with all the juice from the pan. Wisk one egg and then re mix this in with the burger mix.

Pull off a small bit of the mix enough for a small meat ball flatten and cook on a griddle pan. Depending on the size cook for 3-4 minutes., Taste it and adjust the quantities according to your pallet. Then roll and weigh into 2 equal balls. Keep rolling ass large meat balls and flatten after 3 minutes of rolling or until firm.
Once rolled place on some baking paper and leave in the fridge for 4 hours.
Remove from the fridge and leave at room temperature for 15 minutes. pre heat an oven at 180° / gas mark 4. Heat a griddle pan. Once hot seal your burger on both sides leave in the pan and place the pan in the oven for 12-14 minutes. Whilst this is cooking toast the inside of your bun, grill your halloumi. Add lettuce, sweet chili sauce and kewpie mayonnaise to the bun. Eat and the sleep

CHUNKY VENNISON CHILI

SERVES: 4 ≈ COOK: 3 HOURS ≈ PREP: 15 MINUTES

This is a fantastic winter warmer. I regally supply the catering at a carol concert at a local golf club and every year pull this one out the bag. I used to cook chunky beef chili for a company I worked with in tower bridge when we did night shoot catering and combined my love for venison with this. They are both very similar products I keep the venison slightly milder, so the heat is more subtle. I find it cooks better when finished in an oven. Where beef chuck you can knock around in a saucepan from start to finish. For some reason the venison cooks better on a slow and consistent heat.

TIP: When slow cooking add 100ml of stock every hour to keep it moist

900g of diced venison
3 tbsp of vegetable oil
2 large Onions
1 tbsp of garlic puree
2 tbsp of smoked paprika
1 tsp of cayenne pepper
Handful of finely sliced coriander stalks
Half a bunch of thyme
800g of tinned tomatoes
2 green chillies (deseeded and finely diced)
2 tbsp of honey
2 tbsp of red currant jelly
1 scotch bonnet pepper pierced
2 fresh bay leaves
5 tbsp of plain flour
2 cups of thick rich beef stock
4 cup of strong red wine
2 tbsp of salt and pepper

Pre heat a heavy based saucepan with 2 tbsp of vegetable oil add the onions, and sweat until soft, add the garlic puree and coriander stalks and sliced green chillies and sweat off for 2 minutes. Then add the paprika and cayenne pepper. The slowly add your venison stir until brown all over and add the flour, salt and pepper and mix thoroughly. Turn down the heat then add the chopped tomatoes and stir. Add the beef stock and stir.
Then turn off the heat.

Pre heat the oven to 150° / gas mark 3

Take a deep oven tray and pour the stew into it add the red wine, bay leaves and thyme. Take your scotch bonnet pepper and make some small pierces in it about 4-5 and place in the tray.
Cover in foil and place in the oven for 3 hours. Every hour removes from the oven and stir. For the last hour stir in the honey and red currant jelly, remove the foil and turn up the temperature to 170° / gas mark 4
After 3 hours remove from the oven and leave relax for 10 minutes.
Serve with either a thick flat bread or braised rice see page

BBQ HOI SIN BEEF SHORT RIB

SERVES: 2 ≈ COOK: 2 HOURS ≈ PREP: 10 MINUTES

It is all about the sauce hear. This recipe works really well with pork belly you may need to adjust the cooking times slightly, but the same principles apply

400g of beef short rib (With fat)

100ml of hoi sin sauce
80ml of good quality BBQ sauce
1 tablespoon of honey
1 tbsp of light soy sauce
Half cup of chicken stock

In the fat of the beef score with a sharp knife. Seal lightly in a hot pan and set to one side at room temperature

In a sauce pan heat all the sauce ingredients slowly adding at the chicken stock until it is smooth and incorporated pour half over the short rib and place in a pre-heated oven on 150° / gas mark 2 for 2 hours every half hour top the beef up with some sauce until you have just enough left to finish it.

Take it out of the oven and brush with the remaining sauce. Shred and eat.

PLANT BASED

CAULIFLOWER AND AUBERGINE BEZULE

SERVES: 4 ≈ COOK: 20 MINUTES ≈ PREP: 15 MINUTES

Cauliflower is so versatile these days the various dishes you can do with it have really grown over the last few years. I get a huge number of requests for vegan dishes with cauliflower. This one I created when I was trying to create a starter for a formal dinner that had spice and jazz. It looks great, tastes great and is unique to our business

TIP: Substitute the yogurt to coconut milk to make it vegan friendly

1 small head of cauliflower
1 auberge sliced into chips

250g of natural yogurt
3 curry leaves
2 tsp of rice flour
1 tsp of corn flour
1 tbsp of ground cumin
1 tbsp of ground ginger
1 tbsp of garlic puree
1 tbsp of Kashmiri chili powder
2 tbsp of gram masala
2 tsp of salt
1 Green chili (chopped)
Handful of coriander leaves
Pinch of red food coloring powder

In a food processor place, curry leaves, garlic puree, green chill, and coriander. Blend until course.

Then add to the blender, the rice flour, corn flour, cumin, ginger, chilli powder, gram masala, salt and blend again for a further 60 seconds until thoroughly mixed.

Then place lemon juice and the red food colouring and mix in with the natural yogurt. Then fold in the paste from the blender into the yogurt mix.

Once this is thoroughly mixed together slice your cauliflower into small fleurettes roughly 10 pieces and held by the stalk. Precook these in boiling water for 8 minutes so they are soft but still ok to fry

Take your aubergine and slice it into chips.

In a wok heat vegetable oil and slowly place your vegetables into the bezule paste. Then into the hot oil. Cook for 1 minutes on each side.

Leave on a wire rack to drain any excess oil and serve with siracha and garnish with coriander and mint leaves

SWEET POTATO & KAFIA LIME CURRY

SERVES: 4 ≈ COOK: 35 MINUTES ≈ PREP: 15 MINUTES

I made this one for dad at his 60th birthday party. And put a fair bit of extra effort in. All the notes I kept at the time are written below. Fingers crossed you like it to

2 Sweet Potato
3 garlic cloves
50g fresh galangal or ginger
2 kaffir lime leaves
100g Mangetout
100g sugar snap peas
8 peeled tomatoes
2 onions
800ml rich coconut milk
1 Bunch of coriander
1 red chilli
1 tbsp of vegetable stock
1 tbsp of gram masala
2 tbsp of cumin
1 tbsp of ground coriander
4 kaffir lime leaves

Sweet Potato: Peal thoroughly removing all skin, slice into 2cm rings then into 2 cm cubes.
Garlic & Ginger: roughly chop then blend all together add a splash of water here and there to keep it smooth.
Sugar snap peas: Put in a small glass bowl cover in boiling water and cling film and leave for 2 minutes then drain and add to ice water

Start with a heavy based pan about 800mil deep. Roughly half a centimetre of rapeseed oil on a high heat until boiling hot. Roughly chop the onions (quite chunky) add to the oil and turn down to low temperature.
Once the onions have become soft add the tomatoes (Roughly chopped quite chunky) cook of for a 2 minutes. Add the coriander stalks and stir and the garlic past and stir for another minute.
Then add the mixed spices and stir for another 30 seconds at this point add the diced sweet potato and turn up the heat stir for another 30 seconds then add vegetable stock. Simmer for a few minutes add the prepped chill lime leaves then leave to simmer on a low heat. for roughly 20 minutes. Keep an eye on the curry and stir it from time to time ensuring it doesn't catch on the bottom. Once the sweet potato has softened add the coconut milk, simmer for a further 5 minutes (Do not boil) add the blanched sugar snap peas and stir until evenly mixed. Count to 60 and the curry is ready.

Garnish: is always personal preference eating on my own I wouldn't fuss to much but if you are entertaining sometimes it's nice to finish it with a bit of jazz. Coriander, sliced coconut and a quarter of a lime grilled.

Serve with plain or coconut rice

TAMRIND, SQUASH AND RED PEPPER SKEWERS

SERVES: 4 ≈ COOK: 10 MINUTES ≈ PREP: 15 MINUTES

These skewers are fantastic. Great for vegetarians and non-vegetarians all these elements work perfectly together the saltiness of the halloumi and the sweetness of the tamarind bring real flavor to your plate. We tend to cook these over a BBQ, but you can do them at home in your oven really easily

TIP: If you not a fan of tamarind use herb of chili oil

1 whole butternut squash (Thick Dice)
2 blocks of halloumi (Thick Dice)
Half a bunch of Thai basil (Leaves and stalks)
150g of tamarind puree
1 tsp of sweet chili sauce
Juice of half a lime
Pinch of sea salt
Pinch of chilli flakes

First dice you squash and halloumi (same sizes)
Place or the squash on a lined tray drizzle in vegetable oil and place in a pre-heated oven at 180° / gas mark 4 for 15 minutes until soft but firm allow to cool.

Then Very finely slice the stalks of the Thai basil mix together thoroughly with the lime juice and place in the fridge.

Heat a griddle pan or sauté pan and fry the halloumi until brown on all sides. Allow to cool

Then thread the halloumi and the squash onto a bamboo stick alternate each piece as you do. Then heat your tamarind in a saucepan and add the lime and Thai basil stalks. Sautee for 2 minutes

Once your skewers are ready brush cook in a skillet or frying pan for about 1.5 minutes each side

Brush them again with the tamarind sauce sprinkle over the chilli flakes and sea salt. Garnish with remaining basil leaves.

Lush!!!

KAFIA LIME LEAF BROTH

SERVES: 1 ≈ COOK: 15 MINUTES ≈ PREP: 15 MINUTES

This soup works great as a summer starter or a light dinner. You find it quite cleansing when cooked correctly. I created this as originally as a base of light stock for a sweet chili beef recipe I was working on. This can act as a stock if you intensify the flavors

Half a Butternut squash (finely diced)
2 red onions (finely diced)
1 courgette (finely diced)
Half an aubergine (finely diced)
1 red pepper (finely diced)

Handful of Thai basil leaves
1 scotch bonnet pierced
1 Kaffir lime leaves
1 stick of lemon grass (very finely sliced)
1 stick of lemon grass (squashed)

Pinch of sea salt
Pinch of chilli flakes

TIP: Sauté some fried prawns and fish sauce into the broth if using as a meal replacement

In a saucepan boil 500mil of water.

Whilst boiling prepare you vegetables and roast together in the over for 15 minutes. (drizzle very lightly with olive oil before cooing)

Once the vegetables are in the oven and the water is boiled. Place the chili, basil leaves, lime leaf, lemon grass into the water and turn down to a very low simmer. (place a lid on top) leave for 12-15 minute and top up with boiling water if necessary

When the vegetables are cooked remove from the oven. Drain all the excess oil from the tray.

Then remove the vegetables from the boiling water. Pull the pan from the hob and mix in the vegetables. Smells amazing.

Garnish with some sliced coconut and coriander leaves

COCONUT AND CHIPOTLE SALAD

SERVES: 1 ≈ COOK: N/A ≈ PREP: 15 MINUTES

This is a real exciting dish. Full of color, summer flavors and lots of goodness in each bite. Great for BBQs and social events and the beauty of this dish is if you don't like some of the items you can take it out and replace it with something else.

Cucumber (peeled and finely diced)
1 green pepper (finely diced)
1 red pepper (finely diced)
1 yellow Pepper (finely diced)
150g of tinned chickpeas (drained)
2 red onion finely diced
3 spring onions finely sliced
6 baby new potatoes (Cooked and sliced into 3mil slices)
100g of tinned sweetcorn (strained)
100g of cooked brown rice
150g of coconut chunks
50 grams of pomegranate seed
50g of sliced Monge toot
Quarter of a red cabbage finely diced

Dressing
50ml of olive oil
2 tbsp of honey
1 tbsp of whole grain mustard
1 tbsp of sweet chili sauce
200g tin of coconut milk
2 red chilis chopped
1 tbsp of chipotle powder
Handful of coriander

TIP: Add grilled halloumi & chorizo if you're a non-vegan

Prep all your vegetables and place in a large mixing brown.

To make the dressing add to a food processor all the ingredients and blend until smooth. Add a splash of water if to loosen.

Pour over the vegetable mix toss and serve.

STREET FOOD AND SPICE

AVACARDO & CHILLI HOUMOUS

SERVES: 4 ≈ COOK: N/A ≈ PREP: 10 MINUTES

You will find this a Great little snack. Full of vibrant summer flavors simple to make, light and healthy and a completely different texture to guacamole. Is a great dip for breads, tortilla chips and carrot sticks?

1 large soft and ripe avocado
400ml of chickpeas (drained)
1 teaspoon on red chili paste
1 teaspoon of sesame oil
1 teaspoon of honey
Pinch of salt and pepper

Use a tabletop food processor to blend all the above until smooth

PANEER & CHANA DAHL LENTIL CURRY

SERVES: 2 ≈ COOK: 2 HOURS ≈ PREP: OVERNIGHT

400g of chana lentils
150g of diced paneer
50g of fresh spinach
1 large onion
6 curry leaves
1 tsp of garlic and ginger puree
400g of coconut milk
200g of chopped tomato
Spice Mix
1 tsp of mild curry powder
2 tsp of ground turmeric
1 tsp of gram masala
1 tsp of caster sugar
S&P

If you have dry lentils soak overnight. And boil vigorously for 2 hours whilst you make the sauce
Sauté the onion, curry leaves when soft add the garlic and ginger puree and continue to stir. Then add your spice mix stir and slowly add your coconut milk followed by chopped tomatoes once the lentils are cooked add them to the sauce and continue to simmer until everything is ready. Then in another saucepan brush with oil and cook your paneer on all sides until brown. When colored all over put into the dahl simmer for 4 minutes then add the spinach stir for a further to minutes and remove from the heat

Serve with braised rice

SIDES AND SAUCES

HONEY & CHILLI HALLOUMI FRIES

SERVES: 2 ≈ COOK: 10 MINUTES ≈ PREP: 10 MINUTES

Halloumi marinates really well and is very versatile. At out restaurant we slice it down the middle and make marinated burgers from it.

TIP: If you have a deep fat fryer use it

250g of halloumi

2 tbs of plain four
1 tbsp of smoked paprika
1 tbsp of dried coriander
1 tsp a salt
2 tbsp of honey
Pinch of dried chili flakes

Garnish
2 tbsp of natural yogurt
1tsp of harissa paste
Zest of half a lemon
And mint leaves

Slice the halloumi into chip slices / wedges. Mix together the honey, chili flakes and some oil and pour over the halloumi. Leave in the fridge for 2 hours.

Mix the yogurt, harissa, lemon zest and mint leaves and leave in the fridge

Mix together the flour and remaining seasoning. Heat a frying pan with rapeseed oil and roll the halloumi in the flour and fry on each side until brown.

FLAT BREADS

SERVES: 2 ≈ COOK: 4 MINUTES ≈ PREP: 10 MINUTES

What I love most about flat breads is the ease in which you make them. They take seconds to mix and cook. Plus, they are delicious. I tend to have them with curry's, pulled meats wrapped in them or just on their own with a spicy dip.

TIP: Run some flour on your hands before handling

250ml of natural yogurt
250ml of plain flour
Handful of finely chopped coriander
1 tsp of garlic puree
1 tsp of mixed salt and pepper
1 tsp of sea salt

I a bowl add the ingredients and mix thoroughly. If you find it is to sticky slowly add come more flour. Once the mix is manageable roll into small dough balls (or bigger if desired) Then press into 1cm discs a place on top of baking paper.

Heat a non-stick pan until piping hot then add your breads 1 at a time to the hot pan. About 2 minutes on each side should do it. Leave to rest for 1 minute then enjoy.

MASSALA FRIES

SERVES: 2 ≈ COOK: 30 MINUTES ≈ PREP: 20 MINUTES

I developed this recipe after 2 months of being blown away by some chili potato wedges at an Indian restaurant in London. The key to this recipe is the Maris Piper Potatoes the quality makes them so versatile and able to embrace the spice. They are great side or snack and fantastic change from the regular. It wasn't until 2018 and the owner of one of the venues I was renting asked me to provide the catering for his son's wedding and I was quietly confident when he mentioned masala fries

TIP: You can make a garlic and herb place instead of chili one is really vibrant and unique

3 Large Maris Pipers Potatoes

Masala Sauce
2 cloves of garlic pealed
1 small onion roughly chopped
3 red chilli deseeded
1 tsp of curry powder
1 tbs of coriander
1 tsp of turmeric
Handful of coriander leaves
1 tsp of white sugar
1 tsp of salt
150ml of cold water
½ cup of passata
Pinch of flour

Slice your potatoes with the skin on into thin (julienne) slices. Leave in ice cold water whilst you make the sauce

In a blender mix all the sauce ingredients until smooth add the passata whilst blending.

Dry the chips and rub with just a sprinkling of flour drizzle generously with oil and place in a pre-heated oven at 190° / gas mark 5 for 20-25 until cooked

Heat the sauce in a pan and drench the fires in it before serving

JAPCHAE

SERVES: 2 ≈ COOK: 15 MINUTES ≈ PREP: 10 MINUTES

What you get with this type of noodle is the versatility. They are so receptive to flavour. You can marinate them as well if you really want to intensify the dish. Best place to find them is either online or a Korean supermarket. You find a real deep authentic flavour with this dish. Intense in flavour and built up of a lot of subtle flavour.

TIP: Marinate the noodles for up to 4 hours prior to cooking

200 grams of (potato starch noodles) (dangmyeon) (Can substitute with rice noodles)
100g of sliced beef steak (fillet of sirloin)
1 large white onion finely sliced
75g of wild mushrooms
1 red pepper julienne cut
1 large carrot fine julienne cut
50g of baby spinach

Marinade
2 tbsp of dark soy sauce
1 tsp of garlic and ginger puree
1 tsp of sesame oil
1 tsp of mirin
1 tsp of salt and pepper mix
1 tsp of brown sugar
1 tsp of honey

In a bowl mix together all the marinade ingredients. And pour over the sliced beef and place in the fridge. Leave overnight

Prepare the rest of the vegetables cut all the same length and very fine.

In boiling water cook your noodles Roughly 7 minutes. Once cooked remove from the pan and refresh in cold water.

Heat a wok and stir fry the vegetables for 4 minutes (until cooked) then turn down the heat and stir in the beef fry (retain half the sauce until the end)

Then add the cooked noodles and turn up the heat again. Stir for 2 minutes and the remaining sauce and coo for another 1 minute.

Remove for the heat and serve

RICE AND PEAS

SERVES: 2 ≈ COOK: 20 MINUTES ≈ PREP: 5 MINUTES

Another favourite from aunties table. As a junior apprentice I struggled with rice especially flavoured rice but loved it. I couldn't live without it. To be honest especially rice and peas or rice with kidney beans as my wife would say don't think I would want to live without it

TIP: Leave the rice to soak in cold water for 15 minutes then run under a tap of cold water for 5 minutes and keep moving it around before cooking

250g of easy cooked long grain rice (Soaked in cold water and rinsed thoroughly)
350mil of vegetable stock
500g of kidney beans (Not rinsed and left in the juice)
1 tin of coconut milk
1 tbsp of all spice (ground)
1 tsp of salt
1 tsp of ground ginger
1 cinnamon stick
4 sprigs of fresh thyme leave
1 tbsp of dried thyme
2 tbsp of all-purpose seasoning
1 scotch bonnet pierced

Boil your vegetable stock and 100ml of water. When boiled and the rest of the ingredients except for the coconut milk. Boil for a further 10 minutes then add your rice. Stir and cover. After 10 minutes and the coconut milk and stir again. Cover and leave for another 10-15 minutes until cooked.

INDIAN RICE

SERVES: 2 ≈ COOK: 20 MINUTES ≈ PREP: 10 MINUTES

As a bit of a rice nut I created this one around me and my taste. I regularly cook this one for me at home on occasions I cook it at work but only if I'm in a good mood. This is packed full of flavour works well with a mild curry or katsu chicken

TIP: serve with breaded chicken and satay sauce

200g of long grain basmati rice (Soaked in cold water and rinsed thoroughly)
400mil of vegetable stock

1 tbsp of ground turmeric
1 tsp of hot curry powder
½ diced onion
1 tsp of madras curry powder
1 red onion finely diced
Handful of cashew nuts
3 curry leaves
Handful of dry onions
1 spring of saffron
1 cinnamon stick
1 bay leaf
4 fresh curry leaves

Bring your strained vegetable stock to the boil with diced onion and add the pre-soaked rice. The bay leaves and 3 curry leafs.

Leave for 6 minutes and stir again. Then add the turmeric, curry powders, saffron, cinnamon stick to the water and leave to boil.

Then add the remaining curry leaves and saffron and the rice. Stir again.

Then fry your red onion until soft add the cashew nuts for the last minute and remove from the heat

Add tall the and saucepan and mix

Continue to stir for another 10 minutes or until all the liquid is absorbed.

Top with the fried onions and share

JOLLOF RICE

SERVES: 2 ≈ COOK: 20 MINUTES ≈ PREP: 10 MINUTES

I first had Jollof as a child. One of my best friends was from Ghana and dinner round there usually revolved around some amazing meats and a pot of Jollof. It is actually my most favourite style of rice I tomato and hot in spice. There is various version to this you can play around with this depending on your personal preference. I'd suggest black beans and finely chopped mixed meats

TIP: Add chopped chicken or beef (precooked) to the final mix when using the wok

200g of easy cooked long grain rice (Soaked in cold water and rinsed thoroughly)
400mil of chicken stock

3 tbsp of tomato pure
1 tbsp of chopped tomatoes
2 cloves of garlic
1 scotch bonnet chili
1 tbsp of smoked paprika
1 tsp of salt
1 tbsp of all spice
1 tsp of cayenne pepper
Handful of black beans (tined)

Bring you stock to a boil and add the pre-soaked rice and stir.

Add the pierced scotch bonnet, paprika and all spice.

Stir for 20 minutes or until the stock is absorbed.

Whilst cooking in a blender put tomato puree, chopped tomatoes, garlic and salt. Then blend

When the rice is cooked remove from the heat the place in a strainer.

In a wok heat the puree and add the rice in batches and mix quickly and thoroughly.

Add your black beans in even batches whilst cooking.

Make sure all the paste is absorbed before serving.

Serve with jerk chicken.

SATAY SAUCE

SERVES: 2 ≈ COOK: 20 ≈ PREP: 10 MINUTES

This is potentially one of my most favorite sauces of all time. The flavoring various around Asia. You will find Malaysia will be spicier and punchier, Thailand is a very heavy on the coconut and lemongrass and your average Chinese version is very sweet and sticky. Personally, for me its nicer hot but is great cold as well. The recipe below combines a great balance of satay and mixed Asians influences.

1 small jar of smooth peanut butter (basic brand)
2 tbsp of dark soy sauce
2 tbsp of light soy sauce
2 tbsp of sweet chili sauce (Blue Dragon)
1 tbsp of soft dark sugar
1 red chili finely chopped (deseeded)
150ml of thick coconut milk
Handful of finely chopped coriander
Handful of warm chopped cashew nuts
2 tbsp of vegetable oil

Add all your ingredients except the coconut milk and cashew nuts. Turn your blender on whilst blending add the cashew nuts then slowly add the coconut milk until runny but thick.

Heat slowly in a saucepan (keep stirring) or pour cold over various meats

JERK SAUCE

SERVES: 2 ≈ COOK: 20 ≈ PREP: 10 MINUTES

This one is so quick and easy to knock up. Most the ingredients are already in the cupboard at home. Great as a dip of chicken sticks or a light marinade of fish.

TIP: Add 2 tablespoons of dark brown sugar to make into a marinade

2 tbsp of ketchup
3 tbsp of light soy sauce
3 tbsp of strong BBQ sauce
1 tbsp of honey
2 garlic cloves
2 sticks of thyme leaves picked
1 banana shallot finely diced
1 tbsp of cinnamon
1 tsp of all spice
2 red chilis diced and deseeded

Place all items in a food processor and blend until smooth. If still very course slowly add cold water until smooth.

XXL CHILI SAUCE

SERVES: 2 ≈ COOK: 20 ≈ PREP: 10 MINUTES

This sauce isn't for the faint hearted. It's Hot, like seriously hot even as a dip. Word to the wise approach with caution

TIP: Will keep in the fridge for up to 2 weeks
!

1 Scotch bonnet
2 red birds' eye chilis
1 red chili
1 red bell pepper
1 jalapeño pepper
1 tbsp of cayenne pepper
Half a red onion (chopped)
1 tsp of honey
1 tbsp of vegetable oil
Handful of chopped coriander
Pinch of salt
1 clove of garlic finely chopped
2 tbsp of tomato puree

Add all ingredients to a food process and blend. Until fine. Can use course as it is or ideally put through a sieve to remove all seeds and use straight away.

Order our meals online

www.thecraftkitchen.co.uk

Printed in Great Britain
by Amazon